AFRICA
Is Not a Country

Margy Burns Knight

Mark Melnicove

Illustrated by Anne Sibley O'Brien

The Millbrook Press

Brookfield, Connecticut

Tunis
Algiers
Rabat
MOROCCO
ATLAS MOUNTAINS
TUNISIA
Tripoli
Cairo
El Aaiún
ALGERIA
LIBYA
EGYPT
WESTERN SAHARA
AHAGGAR MOUNTAINS
RED SEA
SAHARA DESERT
NILE RIVER
MAURITANIA
Nouakchott
MALI
NIGER
TIBESTI MOUNTAINS
CHAD
Khartoum
ERITREA
Asmara
CAPE VERDE
SENEGAL RIVER
SENEGAL
Dakar
Bamako
Niamey
N'Djamena
SUDAN
BLUE NILE
DJIBOUTI
Djibouti
Praia
THE GAMBIA
Banjul
BURKINA FASO
Ouagadougou
NIGERIA
THE HORN OF AFRICA
GUINEA-BISSAU
Bissau
NIGER RIVER
Abuja
CENTRAL AFRICAN REPUBLIC
Addis Ababa
Conakry
GUINEA
CÔTE D'IVOIRE
GHANA
TOGO
BENIN
WHITE NILE
ETHIOPIA
Freetown
SIERRA LEONE
Yamoussoukro
Accra
Lomé
Porto Novo
CAMEROON
Bangui
SOMALIA
Monrovia
LIBERIA
Malabo
Yaoundé
UGANDA
KENYA
Mogadishu
EQUATORIAL GUINEA
São Tomé
Libreville
REPUBLIC OF THE CONGO
CONGO RIVER
DEMOCRATIC REPUBLIC OF THE CONGO
Kampala
SÃO TOMÉ & PRINCÍPE
GABON
RWANDA
Kigali
Lake Victoria
Nairobi
SEYCHELLES
Brazzaville
BURUNDI
Bujumbura
MOUNT KILIMANJARO
Victoria
Kinshasa
TANZANIA
Luanda
Dodoma
COMOROS
ANGOLA
Moroni
ZAMBIA
Lilongwe
MALAWI
Lusaka
MADAGASCAR
ZAMBEZI RIVER
Harare
MOZAMBIQUE
Antananarivo
NAMIBIA
ZIMBABWE
PORT MAURITIUS
BOTSWANA
LIMPOPO RIVER
Windhoek
Gaborone
Maputo
Kalahari Desert
Pretoria
Mbabane
SWAZILAND
ORANGE RIVER
Maseru
LESOTHO
SOUTH AFRICA
DRAKENSBERG MOUNTAINS

Desert

Grasslands

Tropical Rainforest

Africa is not a country—it is a vast continent made up of 53 nations. If you took the land of the United States and added it to the lands of China, Japan, and Europe, Africa would still be bigger.

From the tiny island nations of Comoros, Seychelles, and São Tomé and Príncipe, to its largest country (Sudan), Africa is the only continent with land in all four hemispheres. Unlike any other continent, it is divided into two almost equal lengths by the equator, and it is nearly as wide as it is long.

If you drew a picture of Africa's landscapes on a large pie and cut it into ten equal pieces, only one piece would contain all of its rain forests. Four pieces would represent the deserts; another four would be mostly grass, farmland, and trees. The final piece would hold all of the mountains and cities of this beautiful, vibrant continent, where several hundred million children wake up every morning.

The sun is just rising as Arim and Efrem get up to prepare for school. They take showers, change into school uniforms, and comb their hair while listening to children's programs on the radio. After a breakfast of sweet, hot tea and bread with butter and marmalade, they put on their book bags.

Their parents gently place their hands on their heads and say, "May God be with you the whole day." The boys kiss their parents' hands and respond "*Yekenielai*," which means "thank-you" in Tigrinya, a widely spoken language in ERITREA. Before they walk out of the door with their father, who is going to his office in downtown Asmara, the boys are reminded by their mother to always respect their teachers and elders.

It is early morning in Palepo, a village in CAMEROON. Before breakfast, Mantoh spends an hour selling fresh milk from the gourd she carries on her head. Tepe washes the dishes while Nkolo and Folla collect firewood and take several trips to the well. Their chores will be complete when there is enough water and firewood for the day. After a breakfast of *pap*, a cereal made from corn, the children will walk to school with their friends.

Classes start in a few minutes. Kip and Arangi know they won't be late because they are so quick. Every day they run several miles to school through the highlands of KENYA. Both Arangi and Kip want to join a running team when they get to high school. They love to run long distances. When they are older, the children hope to train as marathon runners, so that they can compete with the fastest racers from all over the world.

With *pula* in hand, Mapula walks to a corner store to buy fresh
bread for breakfast. *Pula* is the name of the currency in BOTSWANA;
it is also the word for rain in Setswana, a language spoken by over
a million people. Since rain is often scarce, it is very important to the
people who live there. Sometimes babies are named after the
different kinds of rain. Mapula is a name for "mother of rain."

On wintry July mornings, Thomas and his father wrap blankets around their shoulders to keep warm in the Drakensberg Mountains of LESOTHO. *Lehloa* is a word for snow in Sesotho, the main language spoken in Lesotho. There are very few words for snow in Africa's 1,000 other languages, because it never snows in most countries. In Lesotho the paths can be slippery, so father and son use mountain-savvy ponies to travel to the market, and then to visit friends and relatives.

Mona, Basma, and Hala spill out of their homes in Cairo to walk to school on jammed sidewalks. Mona likes to leave early so that she can stop at the kiosk to buy hot, spicy beans and bread for breakfast. The students walk by early morning traffic jams, passing apartment buildings and ancient mosques. If they choose to walk down by the Nile, they would see ships from all over the world anchored in the river's harbors. Cairo, which means "victorious" in Arabic, is EGYPT'S capital and Africa's largest city.

As the teacher talks about their country's history, Abena and Doreen remember the dance they performed at last year's independence day parade. On March 6, 1957, the Gold Coast declared its independence from Great Britain, and changed its name to GHANA. It was the first West African colony to become a nation. Today children in every African country celebrate an independence or nation day.

Chip, Farai, Rudo, and the other children are practicing for a choir concert later today in another part of Harare. They will sing two songs: one about the seasonal rains that help the crops to grow, and the other about the abundance of wildlife in ZIMBABWE. Each song will be sung in English and Shona. Zimbabwe means "stone enclosure" in Shona, which is both the name and language of the people who built the kingdom of Great Zimbabwe about 700 years ago.

The mid-morning sun is already hot when Cyprien asks Justine to help him and the other children draw stories in the sand. They are making pictures about the fighting in RWANDA. They show how they were trapped by men with guns and knives who destroyed their villages. Tens of thousands of children live in refugee camps; most of them are thought to be orphans. Some of the children will be reunited with their families, but for the majority there is little hope that they will see their parents again. Workers in the camp toil around the clock to cook meals and take care of the children.

Muhammed, Safi, and her baby sister do not stand too close to the tired camels, which have just finished a 500-mile (805-kilometer) trek from the salt mines of northern MALI to Timbuktu. Founded upon an oasis, this 900-year-old city has long been associated with mystery and wealth. The valuable slabs of shiny, white salt, about 70 pounds (32 kilograms) each, will be taken off the camels and piled into taxis, which will drive the salt to boats bound for the city of Mopti on the Niger River. From Mopti, the salt will be loaded onto trucks headed for neighboring countries, whose peoples will use it to season their food.

On Fogo, an island within the island nation of CAPE VERDE, Maria, Carolina, and Celso work in the fields. They have milked the goats and weeded the plants. Carolina shoos away the crows and keeps the hungry goats out of the watermelon and squash patches. Just before lunch the children dig up sweet potatoes. They will bring them to their father, José, who has been farming with them all morning. He will roast the potatoes over an open fire and serve them with goat's milk. All morning Lydia, his wife, has been selling goods to her customers in town. She will come home in time to eat lunch with her family before returning to her shop.

Sena, Celeste, and Darine have come to the market in Cotonou, BENIN's busiest city, to buy beans and tomatoes for lunch. As Sena holds her cousin's hand, she greets each vendor. When she says "*Mifonya*," or "*Mifonan*," or "*Mifonday*," or "*Edjidada*," or "*Bonjour*," she hears two little voices repeat each greeting.

The "*Mi-*" greetings are in the Fon, Guon, and Mina languages. Sena speaks Fon at home. It is similar to Guon and Mina, which Sena has learned to speak from friends and relatives.

Edjidada is Yoruba. Sena's grandmother is Yoruba, so she speaks the language well. The French *Bonjour* is not heard as often as other greetings, but Sena speaks it every day in school.

Every afternoon, sounds of kicking, passing, and scoring echo through the backyards, streets, and parks of the coastal city of Abidjan, in CÔTE D'IVOIRE. Henri and his friends play soccer for hours on end. In their neighborhood all the players pitch in a few francs to buy a ball. This time Henri is "keeper of the ball." He will take it home between games.

When not playing, the boys may be watching their favorite team on television. If soccer games are not carried on TV, they are broadcast in ten local languages on the radio.

In her family's tent in the Sahara desert in MAURITANIA, Fatima greets afternoon guests with tea. As she pours the hot, sweet drink, her sister, Asha, watches it foam in the glasses. While the grown-ups visit, Fatima will paint Asha's hands with bright, intricate patterns made from the powder of henna leaves.

Later, Fatima and Asha will share a *loha*, a wooden tablet used to study verses from the Koran, the holy book of the Muslim people. The girls will learn passages by chanting them out loud.

Priscilla and Mary have been traveling for several hours, so they are hungry. They poke their heads out of the window to buy some bananas, of which there are at least seventeen varieties in TANZANIA. Today the girls have two choices.

20

Their uncle has gone into the *duka* to buy them cold drinks.
The girls hope that the man who drives the *basi* will soon tell all of
the passengers to get back on board. They want to get to their
grandmother's in time to play with their cousins before supper.

Every afternoon, Mariam, Oumar, and their friends play leapfrog and marbles on the beach in SENEGAL as they wait for the fishing boats to return with the day's catch. As soon as the boats are beached, the fishermen begin to divide the several hundred ocean perch and red fish. A few fish are given to those who helped to push the boats out into the surf that morning. Each fishing family gets a share of the fish. Even if a fisherman is sick and can't work, fish are set aside for his family. The remainder are often sold to a buyer from Dakar, who shows up in a truck.

Deehab and Makonne want their mother to hurry into the car so that they can get to the National Museum in Addis Ababa to see the "Lucy" exhibit. Lucy is one of the reasons that Africa is referred to as the "cradle of humankind." More than three million years old, Lucy's remains were unearthed in 1974 in eastern ETHIOPIA. Paleoanthropologists were thrilled at how much of Lucy's skeleton was found. Only 40 inches (1 meter) tall, Lucy was a full-grown hominid, and like us she walked on two legs. It is not known exactly how Lucy is related to modern-day humans. That is why it is exciting whenever a fossil is found in Africa— it may provide a missing link to our past.

Tadj and Josephine dig small holes in the sand of SUDAN to play a
game of *siega*. Both children count and toss stones from hole to hole.
Josephine wins because she captures the most stones. Almost
immediately, Tadj sets up his stones for a second game.

Siega, which is called *gebeta* in Eritrea, *tsoro* in Zimbabwe, and
mancala in Liberia, is played by children and grown-ups throughout
Africa and the world. Many archaeologists think that *mancala* is the
world's oldest game. Stone carvings of *mancala* boards have been
found in ancient Egyptian pyramids and temples.

Ondel and Mbo have just finished soccer practice. Even though they are hungry, it is not time for supper. Hot and thirsty, they have plopped down on the couch, sipping from glasses of cool water as they watch cartoons. After the shows the boys and Ondel's sister will go to Mbo's house to eat salted fish with mushrooms, *fufu*, and cassava leaves. If they are still hungry they may go back to Ondel's house for more *fufu* and fish.

Fufu is made from cassava roots, which have been ground into flour and cooked in boiling water. These roots are bigger than a potato. The large, leafy greens of the cassava plant are a delicious vegetable enjoyed not only throughout the children's country, the DEMOCRATIC REPUBLIC OF THE CONGO, but elsewhere in tropical Africa.

26

Thandi and Thato are just home from school in Soweto, SOUTH AFRICA. They stayed after to practice a play about three Nobel Peace Prize winners from South Africa. Chief Albert John Luthuli, the Reverend Desmond Tutu, and President Nelson Mandela dedicated their lives to seeing that all people were treated fairly, regardless of their skin color.

Their grandmother, Nombini, is home from work. She has cooked a large pot of curried chicken and vegetables. The children's mother, Mathabo, and their Uncle Oliver will not return from their jobs in Johannesburg until after Thandi and Thato have washed the dishes and finished their homework.

The alluring fragrance of onions, red pepper, and ginger wafts
through Ahmed's apartment in Algiers, the capital of ALGERIA.
Tonight his mother has steamed and served couscous—the national
dish—with spices and lamb in a big pan. Couscous, which is made
from wheat, is sometimes mixed with honey, cinnamon, and almonds
to make a dessert pudding. As the common plate of food is shared and
savored, Ahmed and his family tell jokes and sip apricot juice.

Chuba wants to get it right. His father, uncles, and grandfathers are watching to see if he is dancing exactly the same way as they did when they were boys. Nearly every evening after supper, Chuba puts on his traditional outfit to practice the ancient dances of the Igbo of southeastern NIGERIA. As he concentrates on what his teachers are showing him, he wonders if he will be one of the few boys his age to be chosen to perform this year at weddings, Christmas celebrations, and harvest festivals. Other boys will be picked to sing and drum.

Aurala tells the first riddle because she yelled, "*Googga*"—"I am telling you a riddle," in Somali—before the others. They are playing *Googgaalaysi*, a 1,000-year-old game from SOMALIA.

"You are in a canoe and must cross the river with only three things: a goat, a cheetah, and a patch of grass. You can take only two items with you in the canoe at one time. You cannot take the goat with the grass or the cheetah with the goat, because the goat would eat the grass and the cheetah would eat the goat. So what do you do?"

With a huge grin Samater shouts, "*Adale*"—"I know the answer."

"First, cross with the goat. Come back for the grass, drop it off, but after droppping it off, bring back the goat. Get the cheetah, but leave the goat behind. Finally, come back for the goat and cross the river."

Hodan cries, "*Googga*," and the game begins again.

30

It is just about dark when city bus number 15 from Antananarivo pulls up in front of the Tsimbazara Zoo. Didier, Charlotte, and Benoit are the first three students to scramble off the bus. They quickly get in line to buy tickets for the night visit to watch the aye-aye, a nocturnal lemur that has ears like a bat and a tail like a fox. There are more than 50 varieties of lemurs in MADAGASCAR. The children are delighted to find that the tiny aye-aye are awake when they reach them.

The sun has set, the children have finished their chores and brushed their teeth, and the stars are shining in the sky over TOGO. Abla hopes to hear the story about market day held each Tuesday near her house. Afi wants to hear about the little girl and the lion. Koffi smiles as his father begins to speak.

"Once there was a wise little girl whose mother told her that if she was home alone she should not let anyone in unless she heard the secret password." Though she has heard the story many times before, Afi's eyes grow wide when a sneaky lion tries to trick the girl into opening the door. But the lion doesn't know the password, and the girl is not fooled.

The children want another story, but it is late and they have to get up early for school. Before being tucked into bed, they will say prayers with their parents to give thanks for another long, full day.

ALGERIA (al-JIR-ee-uh)

Capital: Algiers (al-JIRZ). Population: 30.5 million
National Day: November 1. Currency: Algerian Dinar.

Soccer teams from Tunisia, Algeria, Nigeria, Cameroon, and South Africa competed with the best men's teams from around the globe at the 1998 World Cup in France. In the championship game, two of France's victorious goals against Brazil were scored by Zinedine Zidane, a French citizen, whose family is from Algeria.

ANGOLA (an-GOH-luh)

Capital: Luanda (loo-AHN-dah). Population: 10.9 million. Independence Day: November 11, 1975. Currency: Kwanza

Funge is the national dish of Angola. Made from the root of a cassava plant, it is eaten with fish, vegetables, meat, and chicken. *Muamba* is another special dish: it includes *funge* and fresh chicken cooked in peanut or palm oil.

BENIN (beh-NEEN)

Capital: Porto Novo (PAWR-toh NOH-voh). Population: 6.1 million. Independence Day: August 1, 1960. Currency: CFA Franc.

From the 16th to the late 19th century, Benin was known as the kingdom of Dahomey. Abomey was the capital of this wealthy state, which stretched into present-day Togo and Nigeria. Its ancient stories are woven today into colorful tapestries by local artists and sold all over the world.

BOTSWANA (bots-WAH-nah)

Capital: Gaborone (gah-boh-ROH-nay). Population: 1.5 million. Independence Day: September 30, 1966. Currency: Pula.

One hundred thebe equal 1 pula, and 5 pula equal about 1 U.S. dollar. In addition to being the nation's currency, pula (as rain) is also the national motto. The blue stripes on the flag represent rainwater.

BURKINA FASO (boor-KEE-nah FAH-soh)

Capital: Ouagadougou (wah-gah-DOO-goo). Population: 11.2 million. Independence Day: August 5, 1960. Currency: CFA Franc.

Until 1984, Burkina Faso was called Upper Volta, after the headwaters of the Volta rivers. Burkina Faso is a Mossi phrase that means "land of honorable people."

BURUNDI (boo-RUN-dee)

Capital: Bujumbura (boo-jum-BOO-rah). Population: 5.5 million. Independence Day: July 1, 1962. Currency: Burundi Franc.

Burundi lies two degrees below the equator in the Great Rift Valley. This series of deep cracks in the earth forms steep-sided valleys, which in Africa extend more than 3,000 miles (4,800 kilometers) from Eritrea to Mozambique. The Great Rift Valley is known for its lakes, mountains, fertile soils, and fossils.

CAMEROON

Capital: Yaoundé (YAI-oun-DAI). Population: 15 million. Independence Day: January 1, 1960 (East Cameroon); October 1, 1961 (West Cameroon independence and federation with East Cameroon). Currency: CFA Franc.

Cameroonian children and their families usually share a taxi and the fare with strangers. This is called *taxi en ramassage*. *Ramassage* is a French word for "pickup."

CAPE VERDE (CAPE VAIR-day)

Capital: Praia (PRAH-yah). Population: 400,000. Independence Day: July 5, 1975. Currency: Escudo.

Cape Verde is an archipelago of 15 islands, 620 miles (998 kilometers) off the coast of Senegal. Though known as the Green Cape, the islands can suffer long periods of drought. This is one reason why almost twice as many Cape Verdians live away from the islands as on them.

CENTRAL AFRICAN REPUBLIC

Capital: Bangui (bahn-GEE). Population 3.4 million. Independence Day: August 11, 1960. Currency: CFA Franc.

Central African Republic is one of the 12 countries—Benin, Burkina Faso, Côte d'Ivoire, Niger, Togo, Mali, Senegal, the Republic of the Congo, Chad, Equatorial Guinea, and Gabon are the others—that use the same currency, the CFA Franc. Even though the money in these countries looks the same to the eye, there are secret codes embedded in it that bankers rely upon to identify the country of each coin or bill.

CHAD

Capital: N'Djamena (uhn-jah-MEE-nah). Population: 7.3 million. Independence Day: August 11, 1960. Currency: CFA Franc.

Chad's northern sector is in the Sahara, the world's largest desert. Sahara means desert in Arabic; it is about the same size as the continental United States. In addition to Chad, the Sahara stretches through Egypt, Tunisia, Libya, Sudan, Niger, Mauritania, Morocco, and Mali.

COMOROS (kah-MO-roz)
Capital: Moroni (mo-RO-nee). Population: 545,000.
Independence Day: July 6, 1975. Currency: Comorian
Franc.

Early Arab traders called Comoros, "Islands of the Moon." A
crescent moon and stars appear on its stamps and flag. The
white crescent on the flag represents Islam, the country's
dominant religion.

CONGO (The Democratic Republic of the Congo)
Capital: Kinshasa. Population: 49 million. Date of
Independence: June 30, 1960. Currency: New Congo.

The Ituri Forest is about the size of Israel. Like other rain
forests, it has been misnamed a "jungle," a derivation of the
Hindi word jangal, which means "wasteland" or "desert."

CONGO (The Republic of the Congo)
Capital: Brazzaville (BRAH-zuh-vil).
Population: 2.7 million. Independence
Day: August 15, 1960. Currency: CFA
Franc.

Africa's second-longest river, the Congo,
flows for 2,900 miles (4,700 kilometers),
taking the form of a huge
counterclockwise arc, mostly through the
Democratic Republic of the Congo. It
forms a partial border with the Republic of
the Congo. It ranges in width from 0.5 to
10 miles (0.8 to 16 kilometers). More than
4,000 islands are located in the river.

CÔTE D'IVOIRE (coat-dee-VWAHR)
Capital: Yamoussoukro (yah-moo-SOO-kro). Population:
15.4 million. Independence Day: August 7, 1960. Currency:
CFA Franc.

The Basilique de Notre Dame de la Paix, "Our Lady of
Peace," a near replica of St Peter's in Rome, is the world's
largest church. In September 1990, Pope John Paul II
traveled to Yamoussoukro to dedicate the new basilica,
which remains controversial due to its expense and because
so many Muslims live in Côte d'Ivoire.

DJIBOUTI (ji-BOO-tee)
Capital: Djibouti. Population: 440,000. Independence Day:
June 27, 1977. Currency: Djibouti Franc.

Colors on the Djibouti flag represent the two major groups
of people who live there—blue for the Issas, green for the
Afars.

EGYPT (EE-jipt)
Capital: Cairo (KAI-roh). Population: 66 million.
Independence Day: July 23, 1952. Currency: Egyptian
Pound.

The Nile, the world's longest river, flows north from its
most distant source, the Kagera River in Burundi, for 4,132

miles (6,650 kilometers) to an immense delta in Egypt that
empties into the Mediterranean Sea.

EQUATORIAL GUINEA (GIH-nee)
Capital: Malabo (mah-LAH-boh).
Population: 454,000. Independence Day:
October 12, 1968. Currency: CFA Franc.

Equatorial Guinea is the only country in
Africa that uses Spanish as a government
language.

ERITREA (er-uh-TRAY-uh)
Capital: Asmara (az-MAHR-uh). Population: 3.8 million.
Independence Day: May 24,1993. Currency: Nafka.

Eritrea, which fought a war of independence for more than
30 years against Ethiopia, is Africa's newest nation.

ETHIOPIA (ee-thee-OH-pee-uh)
Capital: Addis Ababa (ah-DEES AH-bah-bah). Population:
58 million. National Revolution Day: September 12, 1974.
Currency: Birr.

Ethiopia, which is at least 2,000 years old, is the oldest
independent country in Africa, as it was never colonized. Its
flag dates back to the 19th century. The colors on it,
adopted from the 1950s through 1970s by many other
African countries upon independence (Ghana, Mali,
Guinea-Bissau, etc.), have become known as the pan-
African colors. Green symbolizes the fertility of the land;
red represents the struggle for independence; yellow stands
for the sun, or mineral wealth.

GABON (gah-BOHN)
Capital: Libreville (LEE-bruh-veel). Population: 1.2
million. Independence Day: August 17, 1960. Currency:
CFA Franc.

The majority of Gabonese live in cities and large towns. The
sparsely populated rain forest in the country's interior is
home to several varieties of elephant and more than 3,000
species of plants, among them the okoume, a hardwood tree
that is extensively logged.

THE GAMBIA (GAM-bee-uh)
Capital: Banjul (bahn-JOOL). Population: 1.2 million.
Independence Day: February 18, 1965. Currency: Dalasi.

In order to write his best-selling book Roots, American
author Alex Haley traced his ancestry to The Gambia. He
speculated that he was a descendant of a Mandinka-speaking
young man who lived in Juffure before he was enslaved and
shipped to the American colonies in the late 1760s. Today
Juffure is a tourist attraction; Haley was awarded a special
Pulitzer Prize for his work in 1976.

GHANA (GAH-nuh)
Capital: Accra (AH-kruh).
Population: 18.5 million.
Independence Day: March 6, 1957.
Currency: Cedi.

Children in Ghana know by heart folktales about Anansi, the trickster spider. Anansi always seems to be in big trouble, but often saves himself by using his head.

GUINEA (GIH-nee)
Capital: Conakry (KAH-nuh-kree). Population: 7.5 million. Independence Day: October 2, 1958. Currency: Guinean Franc.

In the "bathing game," children face each other while sitting on mounds of sand they have built in a circle at the beach. At a signal each player tries to land on the next mound. A player is out if his feet touch the ground. The game continues until one player is left.

GUINEA-BISSAU (GIH-nee bee-SOW)
Capital: Bissau. Population: 1.2 million. Independence Day: September 24, 1973 Currency: CFA Franc.

Amílcar Cabral was the key leader in his country's struggle for independence. An agronomist, Cabral worked with farmers, suggesting that they grow more than peanuts, the major crop at that time.

KENYA (KEN-yuh)
Capital: Nairobi (nai-RO-bee). Population: 28.4 million. Independence Day: December 12, 1963. Currency: Kenya Shilling.

On June 5, 1979, Wangari Maathai started the Green Belt Movement in a park in Nairobi, when she and several women planted seven trees. Today the movement employs more than 8,000 women, most of whom work in the nurseries where the tree saplings are grown. About 50,000 women and a half million schoolchildren have planted more than 14 million trees to replace ones that have been cut down for fuel.

LESOTHO (leh-SOH-toh)
Capital: Maseru (MAH-say-roo). Population: 2.1 million. Independence Day: October 4, 1966. Currency: Maloti.

Lesotho is surrounded on all sides by South Africa. The only other two countries in the world that are encircled by a single country are San Marino and Vatican City.

LIBERIA (lai-BEER-ee-uh)
Capital: Monrovia (muhn-RO-vee-uh). Population: 2.5 million. Independence Day: July 26, 1847. Currency: Liberian Dollar.

Monrovia was founded in 1822 by the American Colonization Society, when freed slaves from the United States settled there. Liberia's name comes from *liber*, the Latin word for "free."

LIBYA (LIH-bee-uh)
Capital: Tripoli (TRI-poh-lee). Population: 5.7 million. Independence Day: December 24, 1951. Currency: Libyan Dinar.

One of the world's oldest-known instruments was played about 45,000 years ago in what is now Libya. Archaeologists unearthed a flute in a cave there, and after extensive study they theorized that it was used not only to entertain people but also to lure small animals to traps.

MADAGASCAR (ma-duh-GAS-kahr)
Capital: Antananarivo (ahn-tah-nah-nah-REE-voh). Population: 14.4 million. Independence Day: June 26,1960. Currency: Malagasy Franc.

Hira Gasy is a weekly performance in the capital city that blends dance, song, and speeches. Both performers and audience participate in the daylong competitions, which take place each Sunday. Often young boys perform acrobatic dances.

MALAWI (mah-LAH-wee)
Capital: Lilongwe (li-LONG-way). Population: 9.8 million. Independence Day: July 6, 1964. Currency: Kwacha.

One-fifth of Malawi's land is taken up by Lake Malawi. Malawi's colonial name, Nyasaland, means "land of the lake." Malawi is one of the most densely populated countries in Africa.

MALI (MAH-lee)
Capital: Bamako (BAH-mah-koh). Population: 10.1 million. Independence Day: September 22, 1960. Currency: CFA Franc.

In 1905 the Grand Mosque, in Djenne, was built with *banco*—sun-dried mud bricks. It is big enough to hold 5,000 worshipers. Every year rains wash away its outer walls, but townspeople restore them during the dry season.

MAURITANIA (maw-rih-TAY-nee-uh)
Capital: Nouakchott (noo-AHK-shaht). Population: 2.5 million. Independence Day: November 28, 1960.Currency: Ouguiya.

Mauritania's coastal waters are some of the richest in the world. More than 100,000 tons of fish are usually caught and processed there each year.

36

MAURITIUS (maw-RIH-shyuhs)
Capital: Port Louis. Population: 1.1 million. Independence Day. March 12, 1968. Currency: Mauritian Rupee.

In 1833 slavery was abolished on Mauritius. Indentured servants from India were brought in to work in the fields, and when their contracts expired many of them decided to stay on the island. Today one-half of the people who live in Mauritius are of Indian descent.

MOROCCO (muh-RAH-koh)
Capital: Rabat (rah-BAHT). Population: 29.1 million. Independence Day: March 2, 1956. Currency: Dirham.

Men and women throughout Morocco often wear a *jellaba* when they are outdoors. This hooded robe with long sleeves is similar to the *burnoose*, a heavier robe that is worn by men, usually in rural areas.

MOZAMBIQUE (moh-zam-BEEK)
Capital: Maputo (mah-POO-toh). Population: 18.2 million. Independence Day: June 25, 1975. Currency: Metical.

In the late 1400s and early 1500s, explorer Vasco da Gama sailed from Portugal to the coast of East Africa. He and his sailors were surprised by the wealth and knowledge of the people. From Mogadishu (now in Somalia) to Sofala (now in Mozambique), towns had been thriving for hundreds of years due to an efficient trading system that stretched all the way to Asia.

NAMIBIA (nah-MIB-ee-uh)
Capital: Windhoek (VINT-huk). Population: 1.6 million. Independence Day: March 21, 1990. Currency: Namibian Dollar.

Namib means "endless expanse" in the San language. Namibia's land is not thickly settled because it is one of the driest countries in the world.

NIGER (NAI-juhr)
Capital: Niamey (nee-AH-may). Population: 9.7 million. Independence Day: August 3, 1960. Currency: CFA Franc.

Many elementary students in Niger attend "maternal-language" schools. Students not only learn their native language, but are taught to honor and respect their culture.

NIGERIA (nai-JIR-ee-uh)
Capital: Abuja (ah-BOO-jah). Population: 110.5 million. Independence Day: October 1, 1960. Currency: Naira.

Nigerian poet and novelist Chinua Achebe has seen his book *Things Fall Apart* (1958) translated into more than forty languages. Wole Soyinka, a writer who was jailed from 1967 to 1969 for his political beliefs, won the Nobel Prize for Literature in 1986.

RWANDA (roo-WAHN-dah)
Capital: Kigali (kih-GAH-lee). Population: 7.9 million. Independence Day: July 1, 1962. Currency: Rwanda Franc.

At least a million people were murdered, and more than two million displaced, during the Rwandan Civil War in 1994. Today, as the Rwandans continue to rebuild their cities, towns, and farms, they are trying to figure out how the guilty should be punished, and how the survivors, including orphans, should be helped.

SÃO TOMÉ AND PRÍNCIPE (sah-toh-MAY and PRIN-si-pee)
Capital: São Tomé. Population: 150,000. Independence Day: July 12, 1975. Currency: Dobra.

In the early 1490s about two thousand Jewish children were forced to leave Portugal and were taken to São Tomé and Príncipe. The Portuguese wanted to populate the island and raise the children as Christians.

SENEGAL (seh-ni-GAHL)
Capital: Dakar (dah-KAHR). Population: 8.7 million. Independence Day: April 4, 1960. Currency: CFA Franc.

Ile de Gorée (Gorée Island) is known as the "Door of No Return." It is 2 miles (3 kilometers) east of Dakar. Slaves were shipped there from all over West Africa in the 1600s and 1700s, then forced onto ships sailing to the Americas, never to return to their homes or families. Today Gorée Island is a museum. Visitors come to remember all those who were forced into slavery.

SEYCHELLES (say-SHELZ)
Capital: Victoria. Population: 78,000. Independence Day: January 29, 1976. Currency: Seychelles Rupee.

The Seychelles is home to the exotic *coco de mer* (sea coconut). The fruit of this palm tree takes seven years to grow and weighs between 30 and 40 pounds (14 and 18 kilograms). Some of these coconuts float with the Indian Ocean currents to distant lands, where they are recovered and eaten.

SIERRA LEONE (see-EHR-ruh lee-OHN)
Capital: Freetown. Population 5 million. Independence Day: April 27, 1961. Currency: Leone.

Freetown was founded by 400 black settlers who came from England in 1787. They were joined later by former slaves from Jamaica and Nova Scotia who had fought with the British during the U.S. Revolutionary War. All told, several hundred thousand slaves, liberated by the British and others, eventually settled in Freetown.

SOMALIA (soh-MAH-lee-yah)
Capital: Mogadishu (moh-gah-DEE-shoo). Population: 6.8 million. Independence Day: July 1, 1960. Currency: Somali Shilling.

At birth, a child in Somalia is given not only a personal name but also the name of his father, his grandfather, his great grandfather, and his clan. However, since their names are so long, Somalis rarely use all of them.

SOUTH AFRICA
Capital: Pretoria (prih-TAWR-ee-uh). Population: 42.8 million. Freedom Day: April 27, 1974. Currency: Rand.

In 1993, Nelson Mandela shared the Nobel Prize for Peace with then-President F.W. de Klerk for their joint efforts to end apartheid and to bring majority rule to South Africa.

SUDAN (soo-DAN)
Capital: Khartoum (kahr-TOOM). Population: 33.5 million. Independence Day: January 1, 1956. Currency: Sudanese Dinar.

A Dinka boy in Sudan is given his first ox when he is 12. It is called his "song ox" because he is expected to compose a song about it.

SWAZILAND (SWAH-zee-land)
Capital: Mbabane (uhm-bah-BAH-nay). Population: 906,000. Independence Day: September 6, 1968. Currency: Lilangeni.

Swaziland is ruled by a *Ngwenyama*, a king. He is assisted by a council of ministers and a legislature. The *Ndlovukazi*, the king's mother, is in charge of national rituals.

TANZANIA (tahn-zah-NEE-ah)
Capital: Dar es Salaam (dahr-es-sah-LAHM). Population: 31.5 million. Independence Day: December 9, 1961. Currency: Tanzania Shilling.

Serengeti, which means "endless plain" in the Maa language, is the name of a wildlife park in Tanzania. This vast park, about the size of Connecticut, is one of 46 World Heritage Sites in Africa. These areas were chosen by the United Nations because their natural or architectural beauty needs to be protected.

TOGO (TOH-go)
Capital: Lomé (loh-MAY). Population: 4.3 million. Independence Day: April 27, 1960. Currency: CFA Franc.

Two-story earthen homes, originally meant as protection from attack, are built in northern Togo by the Batammaliba, who are also called the Tamberma. The name Batammaliba means "those who are the real architects of the earth."

TUNISIA (too-NEE-zhuh)
Capital: Tunis (TOO-nis). Population: 9.3 million. Independence Day: March 20, 1956. Currency: Tunisian Dinar.

During the 7th century, when the Arab conquerors went to the continent of Africa, they called Tunisia, *Ifriqyya*. The word "Africa" is thought to be derived from this. It may have also come from the word *afar*, an Arabic word for "land," or it may be derived from *faraqqa*, a Carthaginian word meaning "colony."

UGANDA (yoo-GAHN-dah)
Capital: Kampala (kahm-PAH-lah). Population: 20.7 million. Independence Day: October 9, 1962. Currency: Uganda Shilling.

Lake Victoria is the world's second-largest freshwater lake (only Lake Superior is bigger), covering one-sixth of Uganda and parts of Kenya and Tanzania. More than 200 species of tropical fish live in it.

WESTERN SAHARA
Capital: El Aaiún. Population: 265,000. Independence Day: not applicable. Currency: Moroccan Dirham.

Though controlled by Morocco since 1979, and therefore not yet an independent nation, Western Sahara is sometimes counted as Africa's 54th country. Using self-government as the criteria for nationhood, we refer to 53 African countries on page 1, though the map shows the border between Western Sahara and Morocco.

ZAMBIA (ZAM-bee-ah)
Capital: Lusaka (loo-SAH-kah). Population: 8.5 million. Independence Day: October 24, 1964. Currency: Kwacha.

The H-P Women's Development Corporation, which was founded in 1989, is a female owned and run corporation that was named after its founder, Tsitsi Himuyanga-Phiri, a women's rights lawyer. It loans money to Zambian women so that they can start small businesses.

ZIMBABWE (zim-BAHB-way)
Capital: Harare (hah-RAH-ray). Population: 11.7 million. Independence Day: April 18, 1980. Currency: Zimbabwe Dollar.

Though now uninhabited, the stone walls of Great Zimbabwe still stand. These ruins are visited by people from all over the world as a way to learn firsthand about Shona history.

Dedicated to:

la famille Gnidehoue (MBK);
Denise and Damian (MM);
Meikie Jenness and family (ASO).

Design: Susan Sherman, Ars Agassiz, Cambridge, Massachusetts
Printed in the United States of America.
First Edition
5 4 3 2 1

Library of Congress Cataloging-in-Publication Data

Knight, Margy Burns.
Africa is not a country / Margy Burns Knight, Mark Melnicove ;
illustrated by Anne Sibley O'Brien.
    p. cm.
 Includes index.
 Summary: Demonstrates the diversity of the African continent by describing daily life in
some of its fifty-three nations.
ISBN 0-7613-1266-8 (lib. bdg.)
1. Africa—Juvenile literature. 2. Africa— Civilization—Juvenile literature. [1. Africa—
Social life and customs.] I. O'Brien, Anne Sibley. II. Melnicove, Mark. III. Title.
DT22 .K57 2000
960—dc21   00-022205

The Millbrook Press, Inc.
2 Old New Milfrod Road
Brookfield, Connecticut 06804

ACKNOWLEDGMENTS:

With deep appreciation to all those who shared their expertise and stories of African childhoods:
Simeon Alloding, Mohamed and Radia Gheraissa, Ahmed Hassan, Sylvanus Jackson, Meikie Jenness, E'nkul Kanakan, Margaret Lado, Metycaine Mntuyedwa and family, Oscar Mokeme, Penjami Mphepo, Thandi Nkosi, Brigitte Nyada and family, Mutima Peter, Efrem Weldemichael, Kokou Yetongnon, Catherine Yomoah, and Aster Zaoude.

To Edgard Gnidehoue for his guidance, to Daria Burns for her research assistance, and to Barbara Brown for her knowledge.

And to all those who helped us along the way: The African Studies Center at Boston University (Africa@bu.edu), Charlotte Agell, Dale Barrett, Bates College, Mara Burns, Toni Buzzeo, Jo Coyne, Meri Nana-Ama Danquah, Mirjam de Bruijn, DeWolfe Family, Mansour El-Alwi, Paul Fredrick, Val Hart, Jay Hoffman, Emilie Knight, Steve Knight, Jane Kurtz, Agnes Leslie, Ann Lynch, Marguerite MacDonald, the McPhedran Family, Cathy Murray, Marcia Nash, Katie Norton, Robert O'Brien, Yunhee O'Brien, Melissa Orth, Pam Osborn, George Packer, the Peace Corps, Jim Perkins, Portland Public Library and Peaks Island Branch, the Reinsboroughs, John and Jean Sibley, Norman R. Sibley, Peg Snyder, Carol Stahl, Pat Stanton, Elizabeth Stover, Rachel Talbot-Ross, UM-Orono, Grace Valenzuela, Gretchen Walsh, Dianne Webb, Cathy Wimette, Winthrop Grade School, and Winthrop High School French IV class.

Although every effort has been made to make this book as accurate as possible, some facts are in dispute, even by experts. The diversity, complexity, and constantly changing nature of the African continent means that new information is always arising.